Koalas

Of all Australia's incredi[ble] animals, the little Koala is proba[bly] the most attractive and best kno[wn] to the outside world. It is so uniq[ue] that it has been given a fam[ily] name of its own — "Phascola[rc]tidae". Sometimes this little m[ar]supial mammal is incorrec[tly] known as a Koala Bear, but it is [in] fact, no relation to the bear fam[ily]. In their natural state, Koalas ten[d to] be solitary and it is more comm[on] to see either a mother with her ba[by] or a single Koala rather than [a] group or family.

Eating Habits

There are many different eucalypts
comprise the Koala's main diet and
ences vary from State to State an
among different animals in the same
Large quantities of leaves (approx. 1k
are consumed, with peak feeding time
two hours after sunset. To assist di
the Koala has the longest known
(about 2m.) of any animal.

Under normal conditions, they have
for ground water and receive sufficie
ture from gum leaves and dew, a cha
tic which undoubtedly was known
Aborigines.

the Northern Koala

There are obvious differences tween Koalas of the North those of the South. The main ference is that of size, the north Koala being considerably sma than his southern cousin. Also skull is smaller and fur shorter. Although fur colours of Koalas v considerably even in the same ony, as a general rule the north Koala has paler and smoother than the shaggy coat of the m robust southern Koala.

Photos: Courtesy of Lone Pine Sanctuar

Research

Research by appropriate bodies
carried out in Queensland, Ne
South Wales and Victoria to ke
track of breeding succes
diseases and general biolog
Multi-coloured tags help to a
cumulate sequential informati
on individuals and some Koalas a
fitted with radio transmitters f
easy location.

Photos here show various aspec
of research. The picture at top rig
shows the large lactating teat use
by the growing baby in the pouc
there is also a second smaller te
for use by the incoming new-bor
The remarkable porcipate har
structure (two fingers working o
posite the other three) is shown
bottom right.

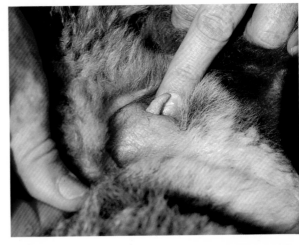

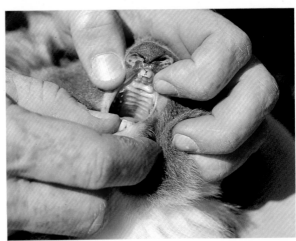

Breeding

Koalas generally breed every ye[ar] mating during warm summer m[on]ths with gestation period last[ing] about 35 days. Males are p[oly]gamous and their mates lead a v[ery] solitary existence whilst carry[ing] their young.

The new-born is minute — bar[ely] 20mm. long and weighing about [2] grams. The little creature strugg[les] through the mother's fur to [the] pouch where it remains for ab[out] six months until well furred a[nd] about 18cm. long. The pouch is [re]markable in that it opens dow[n]wards and sideways and, desp[ite] the two nipples, twins are rare. T[he] young Koala stays with its moth[er] until about 12 months old.

Growth

The association between mot[her]
and baby is very close indeed a[nd]
for the first 12 months, they are [vir-]
tually never apart. This bond of l[ov-]
ing care and trust is one of t[he]
many appealing aspects of Koal[as.]
When about 12 months old, t[he]
baby separates from his mot[her]
and goes his own way. Female s[ex-]
ual maturity comes in the th[ird]
year, when the life cycle sta[rts]
again with mating in the wa[rm]
summer months.

Life span in natural conditions c[an]
be 10 years and in good zoologi[cal]
colonies the Koala may live to t[he]
grand old age of 18 years.